delicious diabetic recipes

Tempting Main Dishes

tempting main dishes

Teriyaki Salmon with Asian Slaw

  3 tablespoons reduced-sodium teriyaki sauce, divided
  2 salmon fillets with skin (about 4 to 5 ounces each)
2½ cups coleslaw mix
  1 cup snow peas, cut into thin strips
 ½ cup thinly sliced radishes
  2 tablespoons orange marmalade
  1 teaspoon dark sesame oil

1. Preheat broiler or prepare grill for direct cooking. Spoon 1½ tablespoons teriyaki sauce over top of fillets. Let stand while preparing vegetable mixture.

2. Combine coleslaw mix, snow peas and radishes in large bowl. Whisk remaining 1½ tablespoons teriyaki sauce, marmalade and sesame oil in small bowl. Add to coleslaw mixture; toss to coat.

3. Broil salmon 4 to 5 inches from heat source 6 to 10 minutes or until center is opaque and fish just begins to flake when tested with a fork. Or grill, flesh side down, over medium heat.

4. Transfer coleslaw mixture to serving plates; serve with salmon.

Makes 2 servings

Nutrients per Serving: 1 salmon fillet with about 2 cups slaw
Calories: 370, **Calories from Fat:** 43%, **Total Fat:** 18g,
Saturated Fat: 3g, **Cholesterol:** 60mg, **Sodium:** 490mg,
Carbohydrate: 26g, **Fiber:** 4g, **Protein:** 26g

Dietary Exchanges: 2 Vegetable, 1 Starch, 3½ Meat, 2½ Fat

Thai Curry Stir-Fry

½ cup fat-free reduced-sodium chicken broth
2 teaspoons cornstarch
2 teaspoons reduced-sodium soy sauce
1½ teaspoons curry powder
⅛ teaspoon red pepper flakes
3 green onions, sliced
2 cloves garlic, minced
2 cups broccoli florets
⅔ cup sliced carrots
1½ teaspoons olive oil
6 ounces boneless skinless chicken breasts,
     cut into bite-size pieces
⅔ cup hot cooked rice, prepared without salt

1. Combine broth, cornstarch, soy sauce, curry powder and red pepper flakes in medium bowl; set aside.

2. Spray nonstick wok or large skillet with nonstick cooking spray; heat over medium-high heat. Add green onions and garlic; cook and stir 1 minute. Transfer to small bowl; set aside.

3. Add broccoli and carrots to wok; cook and stir 2 to 3 minutes or until crisp-tender. Add to green onions in bowl; set aside.

4. Heat oil in wok; add chicken. Cook and stir 2 to 3 minutes or until cooked through. Stir in broth mixture. Cook and stir until sauce comes to a boil and thickens slightly. Return all vegetables to wok; cook and stir until heated through. Serve over rice.   *Makes 2 servings*

Nutrients per Serving: ½ of total recipe
Calories: 273, **Calories from Fat:** 20%, **Total Fat:** 6g,
Saturated Fat: 1g, **Cholesterol:** 57mg, **Sodium:** 308mg,
Carbohydrate: 27g, **Fiber:** 5g, **Protein:** 28g

Dietary Exchanges: 2 Vegetable, 1 Starch, 3 Meat

Ravioli with Tomato Pesto

4 ounces frozen cheese ravioli
1¼ cups coarsely chopped plum tomatoes
¼ cup fresh basil leaves
2 teaspoons pine nuts
2 teaspoons olive oil
¼ teaspoon salt
⅛ teaspoon black pepper
1 tablespoon grated Parmesan cheese

1. Cook ravioli according to package directions; drain.

2. Meanwhile, combine tomatoes, basil, pine nuts, oil, salt and pepper in food processor; process using on/off pulses just until ingredients are chopped. Serve sauce over hot cooked ravioli. Sprinkle with cheese. *Makes 2 servings*

Nutrients per Serving: ½ of total recipe
Calories: 175, **Calories from Fat:** 34%, **Total Fat:** 10g,
Saturated Fat: 2g, **Cholesterol:** 59mg, **Sodium:** 459mg,
Carbohydrate: 20g, **Fiber:** 3g, **Protein:** 10g

Dietary Exchanges: 1 Vegetable, 1 Starch, 1 Meat, ½ Fat

tip

This is a very simple dish you can throw together in just a few minutes. It's great for those nights you want to go meatless!

Spiced Turkey with Fruit Salsa

1 turkey breast tenderloin (about 6 ounces)
2 teaspoons lime juice
1 teaspoon mesquite seasoning blend or ground cumin
½ cup frozen pitted sweet cherries, thawed and cut into
**   halves***
¼ cup chunky salsa

*Drained canned sweet cherries can be substituted for frozen cherries.

1. Prepare grill for direct cooking. Brush turkey with lime juice. Sprinkle with mesquite seasoning.

2. Grill turkey over medium heat, covered, 15 to 20 minutes or until cooked through.

3. Meanwhile, combine cherries and salsa in small bowl; mix well. Thinly slice turkey. Serve with salsa mixture.

Makes 2 servings

Nutrients per Serving: ½ of total recipe
Calories: 125, **Calories from Fat:** 13%, **Total Fat:** 2g,
Saturated Fat: 1g, **Cholesterol:** 34mg, **Sodium:** 264mg,
Carbohydrate: 11g, **Fiber:** 2g, **Protein:** 16g

Dietary Exchanges: ½ Fruit, 2 Meat

Spicy Caribbean Pork Medallions

6 ounces pork tenderloin
1 teaspoon Caribbean jerk seasoning
⅓ cup pineapple juice
1 teaspoon brown mustard
½ teaspoon cornstarch

1. Cut tenderloin into ½-inch-thick slices. Place slices between sheets of plastic wrap; pound to ¼-inch thickness. Rub both sides of pork with jerk seasoning.

2. Spray large nonstick skillet with olive oil cooking spray; heat over medium heat. Add pork; cook 2 to 3 minutes or until barely pink in center, turning once. Transfer to large plate; cover to keep warm.

3. Whisk pineapple juice, mustard and cornstarch until smooth; add to skillet. Cook and stir over medium heat until mixture boils and thickens slightly. Spoon over pork.   *Makes 2 servings*

Nutrients per Serving: ½ of total recipe
Calories: 134, **Calories from Fat:** 23%, **Total Fat:** 3g,
Saturated Fat: 1g, **Cholesterol:** 49mg, **Sodium:** 319mg,
Carbohydrate: 7g, **Fiber:** <1g, **Protein:** 18g

Dietary Exchanges: ½ Fruit, 2 Meat

Cajun Chicken Drums

4 chicken drumsticks, skin removed
½ to ¾ teaspoon Cajun seasoning
2 tablespoons lemon juice
½ teaspoon grated lemon peel
½ teaspoon hot pepper sauce
⅛ teaspoon salt
2 tablespoons chopped fresh parsley (optional)

1. Preheat oven to 400°F. Spray shallow baking dish with nonstick cooking spray. Arrange chicken in dish; sprinkle evenly with Cajun seasoning. Cover with foil; bake 25 minutes, turning drumsticks once.

2. Remove foil; bake 15 to 20 minutes or until cooked through (165°F).

3. Stir in lemon juice, lemon peel, hot pepper sauce and salt; stir to blend, scraping bottom and sides of baking dish. Sprinkle with parsley, if desired. Serve immediately.

Makes 2 servings

Nutrients per Serving: 2 drumsticks
Calories: 173, **Calories from Fat:** 25%, **Total Fat:** 5g,
Saturated Fat: 1g, **Cholesterol:** 108mg, **Sodium:** 254mg,
Carbohydrate: 2g, **Fiber:** <1g, **Protein:** 29g

Dietary Exchanges: 3 Meat

Bacon-Wrapped Scallops on Angel Hair Pasta

2 ounces uncooked angel hair pasta
1 slice reduced-sodium bacon, cut crosswise into thirds
3 sea scallops (2 ounces)
1 tablespoon reduced-fat margarine
2 green onions with tops, sliced
1 small clove garlic, minced
Black pepper or garlic pepper

1. Cook pasta according to package directions. Drain; return to pan.

2. Wrap one bacon piece around each scallop; secure with toothpick.

3. Heat small nonstick skillet over medium heat. Add scallops; cook 2 to 3 minutes on each side or until bacon is crisp and scallops are opaque. Remove from skillet; discard toothpicks. Reduce heat to low.

4. Melt margarine in same skillet.* Add green onions and garlic; cook and stir 1 minute or until onions are tender.

5. Add green onion mixture to pasta; toss lightly. Place on serving plate; top with scallops. Season with pepper.

Makes 1 serving

If there are enough drippings in the skillet after the bacon is cooked, you may not need the margarine for cooking the onion and garlic. Without the margarine, calories are 245, total fat is 4 grams and the percentage of calories from fat is 15.

Nutrients per Serving: total recipe
Calories: 305, **Calories from Fat:** 32%, **Total Fat:** 11g,
Saturated Fat: 2g, **Cholesterol:** 93mg, **Sodium:** 328mg,
Carbohydrate: 32g, **Fiber:** 2g, **Protein:** 20g

Dietary Exchanges: 2 Starch, 2 Meat, 1 Fat

Greek Isles Omelet

¼ **cup chopped onion**
¼ **cup canned artichoke hearts, rinsed and drained**
¼ **cup packed torn spinach leaves**
¼ **cup chopped plum tomato**
2 **tablespoons sliced pitted ripe olives, rinsed and drained**
1 **cup cholesterol-free egg substitute**
Dash black pepper

1. Spray small nonstick skillet with nonstick cooking spray; heat over medium heat. Add onion; cook and stir 2 minutes or until crisp-tender. Add artichokes; cook and stir until heated through. Stir in spinach, tomato and olives. Transfer to small bowl; set aside.

2. Wipe out skillet and spray with cooking spray; heat over medium heat. Pour egg substitute into skillet; sprinkle with pepper. Cook 5 to 7 minutes, gently lifting edge of omelet with spatula and tilting skillet to allow uncooked portion to flow underneath.

3. When egg mixture is set, spoon vegetable mixture over half of omelet; loosen with spatula and fold in half. Cut in half and serve immediately. *Makes 2 servings*

Nutrients per Serving: ½ of total recipe
Calories: 111, **Calories from Fat:** 26%, **Total Fat:** 3g,
Saturated Fat: <1g, **Cholesterol:** 0mg, **Sodium:** 538mg,
Carbohydrate: 7g, **Fiber:** 1g, **Protein:** 13g

Dietary Exchanges: 1 Vegetable, 2 Meat

Tex-Mex Flank Steak Salad

½ pound beef flank steak
½ teaspoon Mexican seasoning blend or chili powder
⅛ teaspoon salt
4 cups mixed salad greens
1 can (11 ounces) mandarin orange sections, drained
2 tablespoons green taco sauce

1. Cut flank steak lengthwise in half, then crosswise into thin strips. Combine Mexican seasoning and salt in medium bowl. Add steak strips; toss to coat.

2. Spray large nonstick skillet with olive oil cooking spray; heat over medium-high heat. Add steak; cook and stir 1 to 2 minutes or until desired doneness.

3. Combine salad greens and orange sections in large bowl; arrange on serving plates. Top with warm steak; drizzle with taco sauce. *Makes 2 servings*

Nutrients per Serving: ½ of total recipe
Calories: 240, **Calories from Fat:** 25%, **Total Fat:** 7g,
Saturated Fat: 3g, **Cholesterol:** 37mg, **Sodium:** 388mg,
Carbohydrate: 21g, **Fiber:** 2g, **Protein:** 25g

Dietary Exchanges: 2 Vegetable, 1 Fruit, 2 Meat

Butternut Gratin

1 butternut squash (1¾ pounds)
6 ounces lean boneless pork chops, trimmed of fat,
 cooked and cut into bite-size pieces (4 ounces
 cooked weight)
½ cup chopped celery
⅓ cup whole grain bread crumbs
¼ cup sliced green onions
¼ cup vegetable broth
2 tablespoons shredded reduced-fat Cheddar cheese
¼ teaspoon black pepper (optional)

MICROWAVE DIRECTIONS

1. Pierce squash with tip of knife in several places. Microwave on HIGH 8 to 9 minutes or until squash is barely tender.

2. Let squash rest about 5 minutes or until cool enough to handle. Cut off top and discard. Cut in half lengthwise; remove and discard seeds. Use knife to score each half into grid of 1-inch cubes, leaving skin intact. Cut cubes from skin.

3. Spray 12×8-inch microwavable dish with nonstick cooking spray. Combine squash, pork, celery, bread crumbs, green onions and broth in dish. Sprinkle with cheese. Microwave on HIGH 2 to 2½ minutes or until squash is tender and mixture is heated through. Season with pepper, if desired.

Makes 2 servings

Nutrients per Serving: 1¾ cups
Calories: 285, **Calories from Fat:** 25%, **Total Fat:** 8g,
Saturated Fat: 3g, **Cholesterol:** 83mg, **Sodium:** 452mg,
Carbohydrate: 23g, **Fiber:** 5g, **Protein:** 31g

Dietary Exchanges: ½ Vegetable, 1½ Starch, 3½ Meat

tip

Acorn squash can be substituted for the butternut squash.

Roasted Almond Tilapia

2 tilapia or Boston scrod fillets (6 ounces each)
¼ teaspoon salt
1 tablespoon prepared mustard
¼ cup whole wheat bread crumbs
2 tablespoons chopped almonds
   Paprika (optional)
   Lemon wedges (optional)

1. Preheat oven to 450°F. Place fish on small baking sheet; season with salt. Spread mustard over fish. Combine bread crumbs and almonds in small bowl; sprinkle over fish. Press lightly to adhere. Sprinkle with paprika, if desired.

2. Bake 8 to 10 minutes or until fish is opaque in center and begins to flake when tested with fork. Serve with lemon wedges, if desired. *Makes 2 servings*

Nutrients per Serving: 1 fillet
Calories: 240, **Calories from Fat:** 25%, **Total Fat:** 6g,
Saturated Fat: 1g, **Cholesterol:** 85mg, **Sodium:** 480mg,
Carbohydrate: 9g, **Fiber:** 2g, **Protein:** 37g

Dietary Exchanges: ½ Starch, 4 Meat, ½ Fat

You can replace the tilapia with other mild, lean white fish, such as sole, walleye or cod.

Grilled Chicken with Spicy Black Beans & Rice

1 boneless skinless chicken breast (about ¼ pound)
½ teaspoon Caribbean jerk seasoning
½ teaspoon olive oil
¼ cup finely diced green bell pepper
2 teaspoons chipotle chili powder
¾ cup hot cooked rice
½ cup canned black beans, rinsed and drained
2 tablespoons diced pimiento
1 tablespoon chopped pimiento-stuffed green olives
1 tablespoon chopped onion
1 tablespoon chopped fresh cilantro (optional)
Lime wedges (optional)

1. Spray grid with nonstick cooking spray; prepare grill for direct cooking. Rub chicken with jerk seasoning. Grill over medium heat 8 to 10 minutes or until no longer pink in center, turning once.

2. Meanwhile, heat oil in medium saucepan or skillet over medium heat. Add bell pepper and chili powder; cook and stir until peppers are tender.

3. Add rice, beans, pimiento and olives; cook about 3 minutes or until heated through.

4. Slice chicken; serve with rice mixture. Sprinkle with onion and cilantro, if desired. Garnish with lime wedges, if desired.

Makes 2 servings

Nutrients per Serving: ½ of total recipe
Calories: 214, **Calories from Fat:** 18%, **Total Fat:** 5g,
Saturated Fat: 1g, **Cholesterol:** 34mg, **Sodium:** 436mg,
Carbohydrate: 30g, **Fiber:** 5g, **Protein:** 17g

Dietary Exchanges: 2 Starch, 1½ Meat

Pork Salad Toss with Balsamic Glaze

½ **cup balsamic vinegar**
¼ **pound thinly sliced cooked pork tenderloin**
   (about ½ cup)
2 **cups cauliflower florets**
1 **medium red bell pepper, cored and thinly sliced**
1 **cup snow peas**
1 **cup low-sodium vegetable broth**
4 **cups mixed salad greens**
2 **tablespoons honey-roasted sunflower seeds**
   Black pepper (optional)

1. Bring vinegar to a boil in small saucepan over medium-high heat. Boil 8 minutes or until liquid is reduced by two thirds and becomes syrupy*; set aside.

2. Combine pork, cauliflower, bell pepper, snow peas and broth in medium skillet. Cook, covered, over medium heat 10 minutes or until vegetables are tender, stirring occasionally.

3. Divide salad greens between two serving plates; top with pork and vegetables. Drizzle with balsamic glaze; sprinkle with sunflower seeds. Season with black pepper, if desired.

Makes 2 servings

Watch vinegar carefully, because reduction will occur very quickly towards the end of cooking time. If it overcooks, the vinegar will have an unpleasant flavor.

Nutrients per Serving: ½ of total recipe
Calories: 242, **Calories from Fat:** 26%, **Total Fat:** 7g,
Saturated Fat: 1g, **Cholesterol:** 45mg, **Sodium:** 304mg,
Carbohydrate: 26g, **Fiber:** 7g, **Protein:** 22g

Dietary Exchanges: 2 Starch, 2 Meat

Grilled Salsa Turkey Burger

3 ounces 93% lean ground turkey
1 tablespoon crushed baked tortilla chips
1 tablespoon mild or medium salsa
1 slice (1 ounce) reduced-fat Monterey Jack cheese
     (optional)
1 whole wheat hamburger bun, split
   Green leaf lettuce
   Additional salsa (optional)

1. Lightly spray grid with nonstick cooking spray; prepare grill for direct cooking.

2. Combine turkey, chips and 1 tablespoon salsa in small bowl; mix lightly. Shape into patty.

3. Grill burger over medium-high heat about 6 minutes per side or until cooked through (165°F). Top with cheese, if desired, during last 2 minutes of grilling. Toast bun on grill, cut sides down, during last 2 minutes of grilling.

4. Place lettuce on bottom half of bun; top with burger, additional salsa, if desired, and top half of bun.

Makes 1 serving

Nutrients per Serving: 1 burger
Calories: 302, **Calories from Fat:** 33%, **Total Fat:** 11g,
Saturated Fat: 3g, **Cholesterol:** 63mg, **Sodium:** 494mg,
Carbohydrate: 29g, **Fiber:** 2g, **Protein:** 22g

Dietary Exchanges: 2 Starch, 3 Meat, 2 Fat